THE STYLE OF COWORKING

Alice Davies & Kathryn Tollervey

THE STYLE OF COWORKING

Contemporary Shared Workspaces

Prestel
Munich · London · New York

Contents

Introduction

In recent years, the important role that the physical working environment plays in allowing for greater creativity and effectiveness has started to be recognised. Nowhere is this more evident than through an emerging alternative work style called coworking, which is set to have a profound effect on what we consider a workplace to be.

Coworking spaces are shared workplaces that bring together diverse groups of individuals and startup companies. The social interaction that happens in these spaces is key to their rise in popularity and the working style that surrounds them. They are made up of people who could potentially work in isolation, in a home office or café, but who understand the huge value and power of collaboration: from chance encounters, conversations over coffee, eating lunch together or being connected through events organised within the spaces or by the hosts of their chosen space.

Coworking interiors are typically informal and have the feel of a café or home environment, where individuals or small companies can benefit from social interaction within inspiring surroundings. These spaces are not just designed for their users to have a desk for their laptop, but also provide arenas in which artists, photographers, fashion labels and designers can practise their crafts. They often have a variety of different spatial configurations for events, workshops and talks, all within open areas where collaboration is encouraged.

Typically, users rent coworking spaces through a monthly membership or through a 'pay-as-you-go' model. There are many motivations for the existence of coworking spaces, from individuals who take on a lease for a space and rent it to friends, to entrepreneurs who see a profitable industry emerging. Big businesses are also getting involved in a variety of ways, from investors basing themselves in coworking centres to Google Campus (featured in this book), which puts a different spin on what coworking is about and who it is for.

As work becomes multilayered and the goal of achieving work-life balance is ever-present, employees will seek to have choices and attempt to work in flexible ways. This will require a rich mix of workplace options that includes your local or preferred coworking centre, as well as your company's office, the coffee shop or your home office. Companies and freelancers will also benefit from utilising the economic flexibility that coworking centres provide, by allowing a type of elasticity that traditional long-term leases do not offer.

Like any culture rising from the underground, coworking comes with its own unique aesthetic and form of expression. In the same way that street style influences high fashion, trends within coworking will come to influence larger corporations and mainstream office workers.

This book aims to inspire those interested in this exciting and fascinating new take on the workplace by showcasing 30 of the hottest coworking spaces from around the world. There is no unified style and look of coworking, and these spaces have been selected to show the diverse range of interpretations that are possible and the inspiring interiors within them. It may even change the way you think about your own workplace and how you work.

Alice Davies & Kathryn Tollervey

SND CYN

Our building is 125 years old. It was originally a lima bean and grain processing warehouse and had been well preserved, with most of the original woodwork and interior structures intact. The fact that it is a historical building definitely influenced the design. It gave us a great starting point. There was so much character to begin with; our challenge was to balance it with some modern elements. The end result is a heady mix of vintage industrial elements and mid-century modern style.

Every item has been chosen very carefully and has its own story. We call our conference room 'The Champ', and there are some really great pieces in there, such as our vintage Eames rocker chair with a leather bikini. I looked all over for that exact design and finally found it in Europe. The coffee table is a vintage piece from a biscuit factory on the East Coast. The hanging lights are a bespoke design that I had made for the space. They're draped around the beams and boards and accentuate the ceiling beautifully.

I love the ball made of railway spikes welded together. The train tracks run behind our office and we found the old spikes in our backyard. Then a friend welded them together. It's truly one of a kind. I found the black vintage pendant lights on a British website and had them sent over. They come from a factory in the Czech Republic.

I wanted to surround myself with work by designers and creatives whom I admire; we have some iconic pieces of designer furniture. I made some of the art myself and some of it was made by other designers. I have an incredible signed Bob Dylan print by Milton Glaser, as well as record covers designed by Saul Bass and framed book covers by Paul Rand.

The uniqueness of the space definitely attracts creative people. We have several photographers and video production groups here, along with web designers and developers and a PR company. It's a good mix. Everyone is excited to be here.

The building is on the National Register of Historic Places, so most of the original features are actually protected by law, which means we couldn't change them even if we wanted to – which we don't. There is a giant grain sieve in the centre of the space that is really amazing. You can climb up a ladder and down into it – if you're brave.

Ty Mattson, Founder

Location	Irvine, California, USA
Founder	Ty Mattson
Size	371 m²
Date opened	April 2012
No. of workers	20

Opposite: Bespoke hanging lights.

Top left: Ball made out of railway spikes.

The building is on the National Register of Historic Places, so most of the original features are actually protected by law, which means we couldn't change them even if we wanted to – which we don't.

Above: Exterior showing the original lima bean and grain processing warehouse.

Following Spread
Top left: Black vintage pendant lights.
Bottom left: 'The Champ' conference room.

MAKE Business Hub

We've used honest materials such as exposed cement and timber, in reference to the grassroots nature of the companies launching from the space. Our use of clean lines, white tones and exposed wooden elements provides a canvas on which creativity and young business can be built. The MAKE branding and wall illustrations are in white, red and black.

The workstations were custom-designed and produced locally, and cater to the requirements of the mobile modern worker. The chairs and bar stools are by design firm Established & Sons; they were chosen because of the quality of craftsmanship and straightforward, functional design.

We are located in a brand new tower in Dubai's Marina area. It's an architecturally inspiring building and our space has panoramic, floor-to-ceiling windows. The abundance of natural light helps to create a stimulating work environment. We left the ceiling exposed, with all its industrial ducts, pipes and vents. The guiding principles were less interference, fewer unnecessary additions and more exposed elements.

MAKE is an important part of the emerging entrepreneurial movement in the Middle East. Our community is made up of young startup founders, creative freelancers and anyone interested in getting into business for themselves.

The Marina/Jumeirah Beach Residence area is itself a hub and we couldn't have found a better location for MAKE. This part of the city – somewhere between business and beach – has an uplifting atmosphere. Dubai is recovering from the world financial crisis and nowhere is this more apparent than in the Marina. Young, forward-looking people are flocking back, with perhaps a bit more realism than before, looking for opportunities in a region that still promises much growth. The very existence and success of MAKE to date is just one indicator that Dubai has a new society in the making.

Clint Martel Wilfred, Co-Founder

Location	Dubai, UAE
Founder	Clint Martel Wilfred
Size	325 m²
Date opened	February 2012
No. of workers	Around 100 each day

Opposite: Bar stools by Established & Sons.
Top right: Custom made and locally produced workstations.

BLINKBLINK

This building oozes character and has had colourful past lives, each of which has left an impression on the space. It was an upholstery shop at one stage and, before that, a pub. When I moved in, I discovered a horde of fabric samples in the cellar – too precious to throw away – and I've kept the old beer advertisements in the entrance area intact.

When we first saw this place, it was derelict and in a terrible state. There were holes in the floor and walls and everything was coated in a thick layer of dust. The walls were painted a hideous shade of orange. I did the work myself with a lot of help from friends, for which I am extremely grateful. We stripped away the plaster to reveal the brickwork underneath and then painted it all white, which was an inexpensive way to transform the space quickly. The floorboards were in a really bad way, too, so I painted them black and white for a striking effect.

To create a really personal feel, I filled the building with precious vintage finds that I've gathered over the years at flea markets, junk shops and on eBay. It's difficult to single out a favourite object from my collection, but I particularly love the Danish office chairs and the retro Riso printer, which I bought for next to nothing from a nearby school. I couldn't live without my vintage typewriter, either, which I use to make quirky address labels.

It's a small, friendly space, so we behave a bit like a family here and treat it more like a shared flat than an office. The vibe is very easygoing and intimate; people here get to know one another very quickly. Coworkers come and go over time, but so far everybody has got on really well. We have two coworkers – Peter and Lisa – who have been here since the very beginning and, as a result, truly 'belong' to the space, but we also have a number of people who join for short periods. Sometimes they just want to use the printer or cut, bind or staple self-published books or magazines. Often, the space becomes a workshop as I run regular open classes and craft sessions.

The location of this building was part of the appeal. It's on Gerichtstraße in Berlin's Wedding district. This is not a wealthy or fashionable neighbourhood, but it's up-and-coming and has a really infectious energy. There's nowhere else quite like BLINKBLINK in this part of town. I've tried to create a place that's inspiring but blends in with the area, too.

Anna Niestroj, Founder

Location	Berlin, Germany
Founder	Anna Niestroj
Size	65 m²
Date opened	June 2012
No. of workers	5 permanent members and varying fluid members

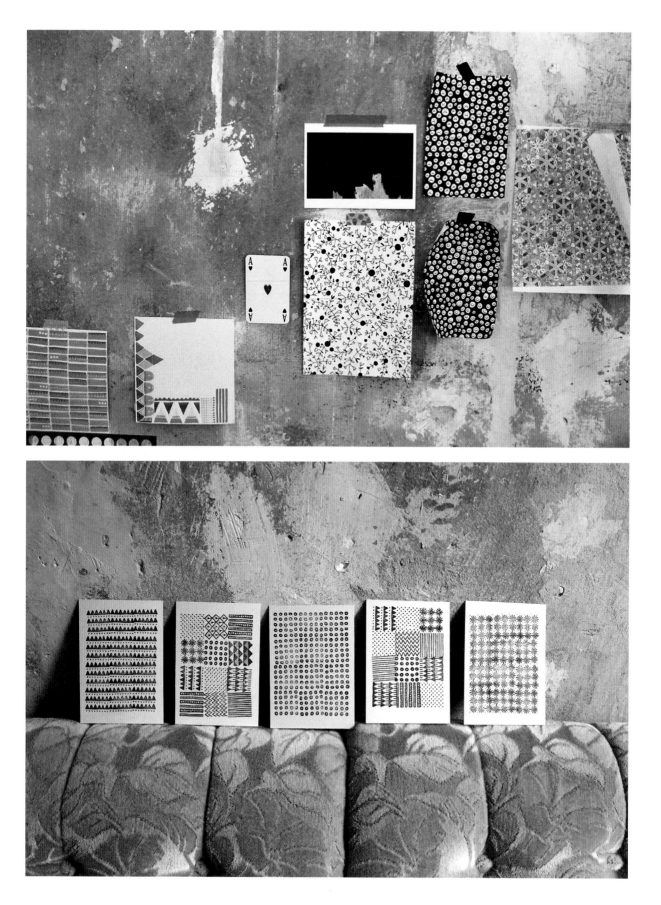

The location of this building was part of the appeal.
It's on Gerichtstraße in Berlin's Wedding district. This is
not a wealthy or fashionable neighbourhood, but it's up-
and-coming and has a really infectious energy.

Top left: Original beer advertisements in the entrance area.

Google Campus

Our seven-storey coworking and event space is in the centre of London's technology district, otherwise known as 'Silicon Roundabout'. Collaboration, inspiration and creativity are core values of Google Campus and we tried to create a space that would reflect and nurture those qualities. Inspired by the likes of Beta Haus in Berlin and Etsy's headquarters in New York, and working with partners Seedcamp, Tech Hub, Springboard and Central Working, Google UK created this space to fuel the success of London's tech startup community.

The design challenge was to take an unprepossessing office building and create an interplay between dynamic, open, social spaces and more intimate working hubs, with flexibility to accommodate a shifting workforce and a diverse programme of events. Much of the architectural focus has been on opening up and connecting the ground and lower ground floors to play host to a series of social spaces, from reception and informal meeting areas to theatre, café and workshop spaces.

The overall look and feel of the building was designed to reflect the nature of its future occupants: young startups who are just about to kick off their careers, rather than well-established corporate companies. By stripping back the building to its core, revealing the existing structure of ceiling slabs and columns, and combining this with utilitarian and inexpensive materials such as linoleum and plywood, a raw aesthetic has been created – not dissimilar to a garage or workshop.

This low-tech environment has then been furnished with several autonomous objects, which emanate a strong presence in the space. In the reception area, visitors are welcomed by a reception desk partly made from multi-coloured Lego bricks – a nod to Google's founders who always had a special fondness for the Danish toy building blocks – in an otherwise unbranded environment.

We have 40 bicycle stations to encourage cycling and a timber-decked roof garden that is used for cinema screenings. Downstairs, landscape artists from The Wayward Plant Project have created a fern garden with flowers that are technologically enhanced to Tweet when in need of water! We have consciously chosen to use a limited palette of colours (vermilion, petrol, lime) to give the building a strong identity.

We like to support homegrown talent, so went for simple, angular, plywood chairs which were designed and built in conjunction with furniture makers at Branch Studios, and chose a huge mural for the café area by up-and-coming artist Luke Embden.

Markus Nonn, Jump Studios, Architect of Google Campus

Location	London, UK
Founder	Google UK Ltd.
Size	2,300 m²
Date opened	April 2012
No. of workers	200 desk spaces, 16 meeting rooms of various sizes, 2 presentation and event spaces

The overall look and feel of the building was designed to reflect the nature of its future occupants: young startups who are just about to kick off their careers, rather than well-established corporate companies.

Above: Mural by Luke Embden in the Central Working café area.
Opposite: Reception desk made partly from multi-coloured Lego bricks.

Following Spread
Bottom left: Shipping container breakout area.
Top right: Shipping container.
Bottom right: Simple angular plywood chairs by Branch Studios.

Jellyfish Cartel

Our building is a converted cosmetics factory that sits right beside the railway track. It is now an arts and innovation complex that houses artists, theatre companies, designers, filmmakers and various other creatives. The kind of people who work here are smart and curious with a great sense of humour.

Today, we still have a few reminders of the building's past, including some heavy machinery (hidden behind a cupboard door) and original concrete floors – complete with paint stains.

We've created a playful interior inspired by many influences, including the original Eames studio in Venice, California, the colours of Mexico, the ocean and the spirit of authentic Los Angeles. Thanks to generous skylights, our workshop benefits from lots of natural light.

When we opened, my friend Jorge gave me some lamp sculptures he made. When he brought them over, I noticed they looked like colourful jellyfish. I had never told him that I was planning to name the studio Jellyfish Cartel – it was just a serendipitous coincidence. They're now the mascots of the studio.

Sharon Ann Lee, Founder

Location	Los Angeles, California, USA
Founder	Sharon Ann Lee
Size	149 m²
Date opened	September 2011
No. of workers	10

Opposite: Jellyfish-like lamp sculptures.

We've created a playful interior inspired by many influences, including the original Eames studio in Venice, California, the colours of Mexico, the ocean and the spirit of authentic Los Angeles.

Opposite bottom: Original concrete floors with paint stains.

DCOLLAB

We enjoy a brilliant location in Malasaña, one of Madrid's most trendy neighbourhoods. Our concept fits perfectly into this innovative area of the city.

Our building dates from 1900 and was used as a karate gym before we moved in and set up shop in 2010. Right from the start, my vision was to create a welcoming, nurturing coworking space where a rich variety of professionals could work side by side. I'm an interior designer, so I was able to really go to town and fill this open, friendly space with many of the details I've spotted in my day job. The finished look is a mix of industrial pieces, chairs upholstered with African fabrics, natural wood finishes, antique lamps and vintage furniture. I hope the overall effect is warm, cosy and inviting.

However, I can't take the credit for our lovely walls, which I discovered quite by chance when I removed the stippled-finish top layer to reveal fabulous old paint colours from previous eras. In my haste to finish the renovation, I almost painted over the walls with fresh paint, but I'm very glad now that I left them in their raw state and just covered them with a coat of clear varnish.

I'm so happy that our coworking project is going well and I feel grateful that I'm able to meet so many friendly, talented professionals who pass through our space or who are still working with us. We have quite a small space, but I much prefer to work in a compact environment than a huge one. It means that we all know one another really well and it's easier to manage on this scale.

Our philosophy is 'love what you do and do what you love'. People who visit us for the first time often say: 'In this building, I can work without feeling that I am at work'. This is exactly what we wanted to achieve.

Noelia Maroto, Founder

Location	Madrid, Spain
Founder	Noelia Maroto
Size	150 m²
Date opened	February 2011
No. of workers	17

The Rabbit Hole

We strongly believe in the advantages that stem from shared workspaces. Ongoing enthusiasm, productivity, stimulation, support and connections are a few of the direct benefits to coworkers – but also, by sharing resources, we're playing an important role in the future of our planet's well-being.

The idea for The Rabbit Hole was to take the elements I loved from coworking offices and little cafés and meld them together to create a hybrid coffee shop and workspace. The outcome is a building that provides the ease and magic of a café (coffee, people, food, books, magazines, a relaxed atmosphere) with the resources of a well-equipped office (desks, Wifi, storage facilities, a private meeting room, studios).

We are part of an amazingly creative community. Our fellow tenants include a letterpress studio, a design studio (Fries Need Mayonnaise) and a photography and digital imaging studio (Ion Design). We all work together to host workshops, industry talks, exhibitions and social events.

This building was formerly a derelict meat factory and when we moved in there were no floors, the walls were rotting and there was no power or plumbing. All of us worked together to transform the space into a functional and welcoming environment. I love the fact that it was a hands-on team effort. We scraped and sealed the walls ourselves.

Our main focus was to build on what was already here and allow the building itself to be the hero. We have consciously chosen to highlight the previously existing structures and textures of the old factory building – we sprayed the original meat racks silver and we use them to hang lighting for photography shoots. We've complemented the urban industrial feel with clean, neutral woodwork to create a balance between old and new. Exposed brickwork gives the space character and makes it unique. As we expand into the building (we've only renovated a third of it so far) we aim to continue to highlight other original features.

I designed the desks and furniture and my husband and his family built every piece by hand. Having created every detail of the space from scratch and involved my family and friends in the process makes this a very special place for me. We get requests for orders on our one-of-a-kind desks all the time.

When we first saw the building, we all responded to the potential it offered. I love the fact that the space embodies a response to seeing possibilities in unlikely places. This core idea inspired the design but, more importantly, it continues to inspire our customers who use the space. It translates into an enthusiasm to get their projects up and running. Creativity and possibility are the main themes of this building.

Dahlia Ishak, Founder and Director

Location	Brisbane, Australia
Founder	Dahlia Ishak
Size	250 m²
Date opened	October 2012 (current location), September 2011 (old location)
No. of workers	14 desks, plus a boardroom and 3 independent studios sharing the building

Opposite: Existing structures and textures of the old factory building.

We've complemented the urban industrial feel with clean,
neutral woodwork to create a balance between old and new.

Top left & **bottom** right: Existing structures and textures of the
old factory building.

the Hive

Elaine and I worked with our designer, James Waterworth, to produce a style that is both homely and industrious. We wanted to take full advantage of the natural light we have in this building. Wood is the predominant theme. All our furniture is custom-made, using locally sourced materials. This creates a space that feels comfortable to spend all day in.

We struggled to get the right finish for the wood from our furniture maker in China. Everything came back too polished, lacquered or varnished, and the concept of 'raw' just wasn't getting across. So we did a tour of timber yards outside of Shenzhen. Eventually, in a ramshackle out-of-town place, we found wood that was perfect – raw cut, local pine, with loads of character. We gave a sample to the furniture maker and told him that was how we wanted the finish to look – just as it does in the timber yard.

The Phoenix building, where the Hive is located, is an early 1990s' office block and fairly typical for the area. It has tall ceilings and windows on three sides (which is unusual in crowded Hong Kong) and one unique feature that sealed the deal for us: on one floor, there was a large unused outside space which we have turned into a decked terrace with palm trees and a seating area.

We have four floors, each of a different size and layout. The interior design attracts people working in creative industries who don't want the Formica desks and strip lighting that is so typical of the city. We have a wide range of entrepreneurs here, ranging from 'mumpreneurs', to early stage tech startups, to freelancers. We kept the original window frames and bathrooms and revealed all the concrete beams that had been hidden by a ghastly false ceiling.

Wan Chai is an unusual area in that it plays host to sleazy bars as well as huge offices, shops, restaurants and many of the western consulates. There are lots of hidden gems on side streets, little parks, a big open market tucked away in a corner, old offices, newly renovated flats, small soup kitchens and big swanky restaurants. It's a fusion of many great things all in one small district. We've tried to pay homage to the urban nature of our location, while creating a space that provides an escape from the madness of Hong Kong. Being in a city like Hong Kong where business takes place 24 hours a day, we allow our members to be able to work 24/7 – just like the city around them.

Constant Tedder, Co-Founder

Location	Hong Kong, China
Founders	Elaine Tsung and Constant Tedder
Size	557 m²
Date opened	May 2012
No. of workers	110

Muses & Visionaries

With loft-style ceilings, expansive windows and eclectic pieces of artwork and furniture, Muses & Visionaries is an inviting and inspiring women's coworking space. It is situated in the heart of downtown West Palm Beach, in the Esplanade Grande building, with a view of the gorgeous intra-coastal waterway. To mirror this environment, we created a workspace that is both relaxed and conducive to productivity.

Muses & Visionaries serves as a curated fine art gallery, which is run by one of our members, Nicole Henry. She features a variety of artists and mediums and the displays are continuously rotating as she buys and sells new pieces. In addition, co-founder and member Lena Hyde, a professional portrait photographer, uses the plentiful wall space for her photography. Guests invariably remark on the beautiful works of art housed here.

We deliberately left the concrete ceiling and pipes exposed and painted them white to maintain the open, loft-like feel. We love the contrast between the masculine, industrial ceiling and the more feminine style of the decor below.

We consciously avoided building partitioned work-spaces in order to create a bright, warm and comfortable area where both people and ideas can flow freely. The floor plan is open with a variety of vignettes that consist of desks and comfortable seating areas to accommodate a range of needs, from working solo to group meetings.

The women entrepreneurs who make up M & V's membership are creative, forward-thinking and successful. They represent a wide variety of professions, including wedding and event planning, design, photography, social media consulting, public relations and philanthropy.

Erin Rossitto, Owner and Co-Founder

Location	West Palm Beach, Florida, USA
Founders	Erin Rossitto and Lena Hyde
Size	371 m²
Date opened	September 2011
No. of workers	Approx. 30 members, 20 desks and seating for 30 to 40 people

We consciously avoided building partitioned workspaces in order to create a bright, warm and comfortable area where both people and ideas can flow freely.

The HUB Bergen

We work in two wooden warehouses that date from 1702 and were originally used for drying cod. In the Hanseatic days, the harbour area was a thriving hub for trade, with sailors rushing to and fro, and now it's a real hive of activity again – an inspiring home for ambitious entrepreneurs. History is literally visible in our crooked walls; in 1955 there was a big fire in the wharf district and you can still see singed marks on some of the wooden boards today.

Because we're on a UNESCO site, there are a lot of regulations that we have to adhere to. It took us four months just to get permission to insulate parts of the building, and when we were given the go-ahead to continue renovations we had to hire carpenters with specialist experience.

It was tricky to make this project a success within such a rigid framework, but the rules actually encouraged us to think creatively. As we had very limited resources in terms of money, people and time, we invited local art and design students to come up with smart solutions for us. Not only did we get a lot of great, free ideas, it also helped to spread the word about our space among young creatives.

In the mid portal of the house (which was originally a lift for moving fish) there is a stunning lamp, a gift from a few of our members. It is made from big bulbs and the cables are gathered together inside a bike tyre. In many ways, it's a good symbol of The HUB as a connection point.

Most of our furniture is vintage, bespoke or upcycled. Our Moulin Rouge-style red sofa was a bargain second-hand buy. We have a table made out of reclaimed drawers and we found our antique gramophone inside the building. It still works, so on Fridays we play vintage records – it feels like being in an old film.

Members either have a fixed desk, a private office or sign up to a flexible time-based model in the main coworking areas. There's a really diverse mix of professions, backgrounds and ages here – freelancers, innovators, or simply people who want to work in an inspiring environment. Many of our members want to make a positive impact in the world and work to find solutions to reduce air pollution, improve care for the elderly or help ex-criminals to slot back into society. This is not just a coworking space: it's an incubator, a project generator and an arena for events.

Silje Grastveit, Founder

Location	Bergen, Norway
Founder	Silje Grastveit
Size	500 m²
Date opened	September 2011
No. of workers	60 members

Many of our members want to make a positive impact in the world and work to find solutions to reduce air pollution, improve care for the elderly or help ex-criminals to slot back into society.

Opposite bottom: Table made out of reclaimed drawers.

societyM

Our space is designed as a modern club for creative people, mixed with a coffee bar and lounge, but is meant for working, meeting and getting inspired. It is located within the citizenM Glasgow hotel building. The concept of citizenM is to cut out all hidden costs and remove all unnecessary items, in order to provide guests with a luxury feel for a budget price. The hotel rooms are all 14 m², prefabricated in citizenM's own factory, then transported and stacked together. societyM is on the ground floor and has a more eclectic style than the hotel area.

societyM was created for a new type of worker: those who aren't bound by offices or office conventions, wanderers doing business wherever the connectivity is good and the coffee fresh. We call these people 'business nomads'. We offer them spacious 'creating rooms', each fully equipped with audiovisual equipment and wipe-clean walls for notes. There is also a screening room for up to 50 people, so you can share ideas with a big crowd. When you're not presenting, there's a club room filled with Vitra furniture, bookshelves full of inspiration and free Wifi. We have a coffee bar, and two work booths are available for people who need to concentrate without distractions. The wooden bamboo floor creates a warm atmosphere and the black ceiling gives an intimate feel. The printed rugs are pixelated digital images of old Persian rugs – a gentlemen's club item modernised. At the entrance, each member has a private mailbox that serves as a safe as well.

In the 'creating rooms', untreated black steel window frames with pivoting shades and second-hand wooden doors again create the feel of a gentlemen's club with a contemporary twist. The corridor in front of these spaces houses low seating, while the screening room has plush velvet curtains and 50 Tom Dixon chairs.

Robin Chadha, CMO and Co-Founder

Location	Glasgow, Scotland, UK
Founder	citizenM Hotels
Size	600 m²
Date opened	May 2011
No. of workers	120

Above: Screening room with Tom Dixon chairs.

societyM was created for a new type of worker: those who aren't bound by offices or office conventions, wanderers doing business wherever the connectivity is good and the coffee fresh.

Opposite: Printed rugs depicting pixelated digital images of old Persian rugs.

63

Top left: Wooden bamboo floor of the Clubroom.
Opposite top: Exterior at night.
Opposite bottom: Booths of the Clubroom.

St Oberholz

The energy here is infectious: even people who didn't plan to start their own businesses get bitten by the bug once they've visited this space. Most of the people who work here are founders of startups or work in the information technology business.

To create our coworking space, we retained the basic design of our St Oberholz restaurant and combined it with highly functional elements. Our architects and interior designers Astrid Pankrath and Sebastian Windisch were inspired by black and white, because the Rosenthaler Platz we overlook is very colourful and has a lot of traffic and movement.

We have two old yellow phone booths in the corridor. They used to be public payphones at Cologne airport in the 1970s, but today our members use them for private phone calls because you cannot be heard outside the booths. We love the bright, cheery yellow. Inside, you can see old phone number listings, with numbers that consist of only four digits!

The house was built in 1898. Before that, it was a Bavarian beer hall with offices above. We've kept the ceiling in the old 'knights' hall'. The name 'St Oberholz' is a reminder that the founders come from Bavaria. The building has a rich past – bohemians used to hang out here in the café and the likes of George Grosz and Alfred Döblin were resident guests. We think it's important to know the history of a space in order to create a revolutionary new design for it that's sustainable but also respectful to the past.

Ansgar Oberholz, Co-Founder

Location	Berlin, Germany
Founders	Koulla Louca and Ansgar Oberholz
Size	130 m²
Date opened	November 2011
No. of workers	22 members and 18 desks

Makeshift Society

Almost everything in our space – from the furnishings to the lighting – has been kindly donated by our partners. Since we didn't have complete control over what might be donated, the pieces had to work as a unique blend of old and new; we embraced an eclectic, mismatched look. We intentionally requested an assortment of unique chairs from various eras (from mid-century modern to industrial chic) because we knew they would complement each other.

There's a big comfy sofa like you might find in an old library, and cosy window seats with a mixture of colour and pattern. It's all very bohemian, comfortable and inviting, like any creative space should be.

We love our vintage lockers. Rena bought them online and we added little fluorescent orange knobs and brass locks so our members can store valuables safely when they pop out for lunch. Our carpenter, Michael Woo, custom-built a whitewashed pinewood frame that houses them, with shelving storage on top. They're one of a kind.

Our building dates from 1907 and has wonderful bay windows with leaded glass panes. Right from the start of the project, we wanted to create sunny window seats for members to read, work and relax on, so we commissioned Chiosso Brothers Upholstery to make bespoke cushions in a durable dark grey denim for us, and we accessorised with cushions and throws from Anthropologie for added comfort.

We kept the high, exposed ceilings and added industrial-looking drop pendant lighting from Schoolhouse Electric to keep the space feeling open and light. A small loft was added to take full advantage of the space's immense height.

Hayes Valley, where we're based, is a thriving neighbourhood with a strong sense of community that attracts a lot of like-minded creative entrepreneurs. I like to think that we've created an accessible and inspiring space that will attract interesting people to work and collaborate here.

Victoria Smith, Co-Founder

Location	San Francisco, California, USA
Founders	Rena Tom, Victoria Smith and Suzanne Shade
Size	90 m²
Date opened	September 2012
No. of workers	175

Above: Industrial-looking drop pendant lighting from Schoolhouse Electric.

Hayes Valley, where we're based, is a thriving neighbourhood with a strong sense of community that attracts a lot of like-minded creative entrepreneurs.

Above: Bespoke dark grey denim cushions made by Chiosso Brothers Upholstery, with cushions and throws from Anthropologie.

The HUB Westminster

The HUB Westminster, designed by architecture studio 00:/, is on the first floor of New Zealand House, a Grade II officially listed historic building in central London designed by Robert Matthews of RMJM in 1959 as a modern skyscraper of its time. It stands on the site of the Carlton Hotel that was bombed in World War II. With its marble wall and dark wood-panel interiors, the building feels as though it was from the TV series *Mad Men*, yet it also seems super light, with floor-to-ceiling windows along the length of each facade offering amazing views on to Pall Mall and Trafalgar Square.

The style was inspired by the location, the existing building and our mission to create a 'superstudio' for the new economy. Since we're housed in a listed building, we retained the original wall finishes such as the marble and timber panels. We wanted to create the feeling of a space that had been taken over by an FBI special ops team, dynamic in its energy, to reflect the innovative startups that are our membership community.

The HUB Westminster is a short walk from Whitehall and Downing Street (in fact the current prime minister has walked from Number 10 to the HUB!). We are next door to all the hedge funds in St James's and also in an area known for its members' clubs that represented many important institutions of the 18th, 19th and 20th centuries. This local history influenced our decision to design the space as a 21st-century version of a members'

club that holds values we feel will be important for our future. We promote ethical, sustainable and collaborative ways of doing business and innovating.

We have a belief in shared and open structures and reflected this in our choice of furniture manufacturing (using CNC cutting). Our tables and WIKIhouse (one of our meeting rooms) utilise CNC technology, reflecting an emerging open manufacturing industry where designs are shared and adapted locally. The WIKIhouse subsequently won a TED City 2.0 prize and is now being developed into housing shelters in favelas in Rio.

Our members are change-makers who are innovating at the forefront of many different sectors, but what brings them together at the HUB Westminster is the eagerness to share knowledge and learn from each other in a trusted peer environment. The space has been designed to encourage collaboration and the sharing of ideas on small and large scales.

Alice Fung, Co-Founder

Location	London, UK
Founders	Tim Ahrensbach, Alice Fung and Indy Johar
Size	1,114 m²
Date opened	October 2011
No. of workers	Currently has 450 members

Lightspace

Our studios are housed in an old warehouse on the fringe of Brisbane's Fortitude Valley. This area used to have a seedy reputation, but now it's the heart of the city's creative industry and the perfect spot for a vibrant coworking space.

We're located adjacent to a railway line, so we tried to accentuate the visual movement of the trains in the layout. In the downstairs venue, the bar was designed so that it wouldn't impede the view, while upstairs the beautiful deck offers a magnificent vista along the tracks towards the city. It's a trainspotter's paradise.

Right from the start we were happily influenced by the building's existing industrial aesthetic. It had fantastic raw elements, including gigantic steel pylons shipped over from England and incredible Australian hardwood timber floors. We wanted to retain these features as well as add our own touches to create a unique working environment. To complement this, we also converted two recycled shipping containers to house the meeting room and facilities.

The upstairs portion of the building was formerly owned by a printing firm, while downstairs was a car-repair garage. The printers had been in the building for nearly 50 years and kindly left behind a massive industrial guillotine that is now enjoying a happy retirement as a feature piece at the entrance to our studios. It's nice to have a link between the building's industrial past and the present day. We've kept the original wooden trusses and floorboards, too – important features of the new space. After 50 years of industrial life, they were covered in thick layers of grime, but we brought them back to life and now they're stunning. We're blessed with high ceilings and plenty of natural daylight, which is vital for a positive working environment.

The atmosphere here is always lively thanks to the eclectic mix of creatives we have, including architects, photographers, fashion labels, graphic designers and PR officers. In an open-plan space, it's crucial that everyone gets along. We have regular barbecues, drinks on the deck, baking competitions and even a knitting class, so there is plenty of interaction between our tenants. There are also quite a few dogs around who come to work with their owners, which means there is always someone friendly to play with!

Downstairs, we have a buzzing boutique event and exhibition venue where we host product launches, fashion shows, exhibitions, photo and video shoots, weddings, parties – pretty much any kind of event you can imagine. There is always something good going on.

John Macdonald, Founder

Location	Brisbane, Australia
Founder	John Macdonald
Size	350 m²
Date opened	October 2009
No. of workers	30

Opposite: Recycled shipping containers to house meeting room and facilities.

Super + Super

We had the concept for Super + Super long before we found this space and when we walked in here we just knew it was a perfect fit. The old shop floor makes a great teaching space and doubles as a stage area for live performances, while the basement is handy for squirrelling away supplies and doing messy work such as screen printing. We were very lucky to get the premises before they went on the market.

The space is flexible and still evolving, so we're constantly adding new pieces of art and furniture as we come across them. We took colour inspiration from 1960s' interiors and have gone for a bright, clean, slightly Scandinavian feel. As a creative hub and craft venue, it's important to us to remain very gender neutral, so there are no chintzy floral patterns – that's definitely not our style. We want everyone to get involved in our exciting classes and events as well as working in our studios.

Most of our furniture and soft furnishings are thrift finds, recycled or homemade. Our two-seater Ercol sofa was found on the website Preloved. It had come from a nursing home and was upholstered in a dingy, brown, carpet-like fabric. On the night that our lease contract on the studio was completed, we celebrated with a bottle of red and re-upholstered the sofa using a fantastic pair of 1960s' floral print curtains that we found in a charity shop in Hastings. Now, the sofa looks great and is one of our most prized possessions.

The building is over a hundred years old, with high corniced ceilings, sash windows and endearing wonky features here and there. Before we moved in, it was a wallpaper shop and, before that, a fancy homewares boutique. During the renovation, we carefully left all the original period features intact. When we stripped back the ugly carpets, we uncovered beautiful wooden floors and tiled hearths. We kept the fireplace in the kitchen, the original curved glass window and a few areas of vintage wallpaper in the bathrooms. The pattern portrays a kitsch woodland waterfall scene and a wooden cabin – it was just too good to remove!

We have a real mixture of inspirational, creative people working in our studios, from jazz-singing book cover illustrators to expert web designers and seamstresses. This mix makes for a vibrant, supportive environment where hard workers thrive.

Claire Culley and Amy Phipps, Co-Founders

Location	Brighton, UK
Founders	Claire Culley and Amy Phipps
Size	81 m²
Date opened	March 2012
No. of workers	10 permanent residents and 12 coworkers

Opposite: Two-seater Ercol sofa from the website Preloved.

We took colour inspiration from 1960s' interiors and
have gone for a bright, clean, slightly Scandinavian feel.

Vuka

Our space is a hub for creative people in the heart of the South Austin district known as 78704 – a key artist melting-pot in the city. We attract designers, social entrepreneurs, yoga teachers and digital artists. It's a diverse group where everybody is passionate about their work and enjoys connecting with other people. The building, featuring 25-foot ceilings, was originally an industrial warehouse used for storing government documents. The loading dock is often open like a large window to let in fresh air and sunshine. The original cement floors are also in keeping with the raw, industrial look. The backyard offers a tranquil retreat in the city for meetings or just taking breaks.

Vuka's interior is inspired by nature, so we have brought the outside in. Dwarf yaupon trees have been transformed into chandeliers, reclaimed wood from local forest fires has been used for fencing, and we have created artistic railings out of scrap wood from a saw mill. Many of our desks are built out of repurposed 1930s' mine cabinets and we've transformed vintage buckets and washtubs into creative light fixtures.

We favour reclaimed and vintage furniture, which embodies the character of Vuka. Notable pieces include Asian industrial carts, vintage sofas and drafting tables from the 1930s. Colourwise, we've chosen a combination of orange (for inspiration) and blue (for calm). We are committed to creating thoughtful environments where dynamic people can gather to connect and create.

Vuka

Location	Austin, Texas, USA
Founders	Brian Schoenbaum, Moya Khabele, Nick Hammond, Jake Winkelman, Michelle Symons and Caitlin Leach
Size	631 m²
Date opened	June 2012
No. of workers	Currently has 65 members

Vuka's interior is inspired by nature, so we have brought the outside in.

Following Spread
Reclaimed, repurposed and vintage furniture.

Creative Lounge MOV

The theme for our lounge is a park in a city, where various people gather together for short periods of time. With all our furniture, whether bespoke or readymade, we wanted to create an atmosphere similar to the one you find in a city park, where people come for various purposes, to think on their own, or to talk with friends. We have used exactly the same kind of benches that you can find in New York's Central Park, and the designs for our separate booths and bookshelves were inspired by the kiosks and juice stands found in bustling city squares.

Our lounge is in a brand new building, Shibuya Hikarie – a 34-floor skyscraper complex located in the Shibuya area of Tokyo. It is the first building completed in a big city regeneration project that will be completed in 2027. Our lounge is on the 8th floor, along with the world-famous Koyama Tomio Gallery, the d47 design travel store (which stocks well-designed products from all over Japan) and a unique event space. The whole floor oozes creativity. We hope that our design, created by KOKUYO Furniture Co., Ltd. and Jamo Associates, stimulates and inspires the creativity of our members as well.

Shibuya is a melting-pot – one of the most diverse parts of Tokyo. Like the city, we have many kinds of members: entrepreneurs, cartoonists, writers, programmers, bankers, English and French teachers, and even corporate types who prefer working in a different environment to their usual offices.

Shibuya has always been a cultural district where trends are set, and creative industries such as music, fashion and design thrive. It has, at the same time, been a gathering place for people who start their own businesses with exciting new ideas. We are here to introduce new ways of working.

Creative Lounge MOV

Location	Tokyo, Japan
Founder	KOKUYO Furniture Co., Ltd.
Size	888 m²
Date opened	April 2012
No. of workers	125 seats

Opposite bottom: Benches inspired by those found in New York's Central Park.

The HUB Madrid

Our coworkers are young startup owners who came together to create a Madrid branch of The HUB's global network. We now provide timeshare offices for social entrepreneurs, who conduct various projects with the aim of 'changing the world'.

This building used to be an old garage. Before that, there was a tramline on this site, linking the two main train stations in Madrid. When we first saw the garage, we got a strong gut feeling that we were in the right place. It was in good condition and had been untouched since the 1940s. The place was like an oasis in this part of Madrid.

It was important to us to create an economically sustainable building by implementing energy-saving features and recycling processes in our design. Finding new ways to re-invent existing buildings for the future and make them sustainable is one of the great challenges of our time.

We didn't want to alter or obscure the rich layers of history here, so we kept our design simple. We installed an underfloor heating system beneath large planks of wood, which keeps the building warm in winter and cool in summer. We left most of the walls unpainted and raw so we could appreciate their flaws and character, but we lined the ones in the meeting rooms with recycled wool felt.

Instead of introducing new elements, we asked The HUB community members to donate unwanted pieces of furniture and we gathered other second-hand pieces, giving them a new lease of life. We wanted to incorporate some more unusual finds, so we bought fruit crates, which can be used as stools, side tables and shelves.

We planted an orange tree in the area where the car mechanics used to change the oil in vehicles. This is a good symbol of what we've achieved here – bringing fresh, natural life to an unloved, industrial space. We currently host numerous events and our building has become a major focus of cultural and social activity in the neighbourhood.

We chose materials that are typical of industrial spaces, such as steel and polished concrete – grey is the predominant colour. Some pieces of furniture come from my grandfather's 1950s' architecture studio, such as the big table, some drawing boards, and desks imported from Sweden in 1955.

Overall, it is a warm industrial space with a quiet and friendly feel to it, where architects coexist with other professionals. Music is played at low volume while we work but we keep the meeting rooms as quiet zones.

HUB Madrid/Churtichaga+Quadra-Salcedo arguitectos, Architects

Location	Madrid, Spain
Founders	Paula Almansa, José Almansa, Max Oliva, Daniel Truran, Soledad Pons, Marina Roveta, Anita Seidler, Lotfi El-Ghandouri
Size	350 m²
Date opened	February 2010
No. of workers	Currently has 280 members

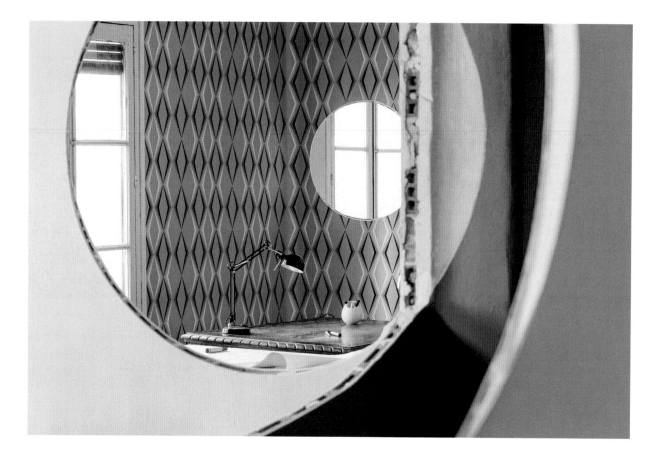

Finding new ways to re-invent existing buildings for the future and make them sustainable is one of the great challenges of our time.

Above: An orange tree in the area where car mechanics used to change oil in vehicles.

Following Spread
Fruit crates as shelving.

The Oracle Club

This building is owned by our good friend, architect Evan Jenkins. He is responsible for the unique layout of the place. We live upstairs, which allows us to come and go as we please throughout the day. The building was constructed around the turn of the last century and the back room, which is now the salon, was once a wedding hall. I think some of the festive spirit lingers in the air.

We've channelled lots of influences to create this eclectic space, from the homes of Surrealists and the films of Jean Cocteau to Whistler's Peacock Room and Cocteau's Chapelle Saint-Pierre. The floors in the salon are original, as are the beautiful exposed brick walls.

The velvet horned furniture in the salon was in the apartment that Julian grew up in. They are 1870s' antiques from Texas and were a generous contribution from Julian's mother when we first opened.

Jenna Gribbon, Co-Founder

Location	Brooklyn, New York, USA
Founders	Jenna Gribbon and Julian Tepper
Size	232 m²
Date opened	December 2011
No. of workers	Currently has 40 members

Opposite bottom: Velvet horned furniture, 1870s' antiques.

Central Working

Central Working provides the ideal environment for growing businesses. We have created stylish clubs that have their own distinct individual feel rather than applying a 'cookie-cutter' approach. We believe each should reflect the locality and its community. The clubs offer members all the crucial ingredients needed to grow, develop and succeed with their ventures.

Our first club is in a hotel and has a lovely homely feel. Our second is in partnership with Google as part of the Campus project and has a very Shoreditch-type atmosphere, while our third is an ultra-slick Silicon Valley-meets-Shoreditch members' club. The artwork on our walls is by Anthony John Grey, one of our members.

Our Bloomsbury club complements the Central London area with its contemporary-yet-traditional style. It embodies the variety of clientele who frequent the space. We are founding partners of Google Campus, where the Central Working café has created a hive of collaboration and creativity. It brings the ethos of Central Working to the heart of Tech City. It is a large, open, collaborative space and this is reflected in our branding with block colour and a large, statement design. It's free to access and attracts over 1,000 businesses a week, many of them early-stage startups. Our new Shoreditch club maintains the chic style of the Bloomsbury club, yet is slightly more artsy, which appeals to the local East London audience.

Central Working provides the ideal environment for startups. We offer our members the support, infrastructure and tools needed to create the connections, momentum and recognition that will grow their businesses. Without being exclusive, we allow people to push through boundaries by offering inspiration, encouragement and opportunities for collaboration. Our members come from a wide range of backgrounds – from design to technology startups – so we are always surrounded by a wealth of rich and varied knowledge.

Central Working

Location	London, UK
Founders	James Layfield and Steve Pette
Size	353 m² (Bloomsbury); 450 m² (Campus); 344 m² (Shoreditch)
Date opened	April 2011 (Bloomsbury); April 2012 (Campus); November 2012 (Shoreditch)
No. of workers	1,500 weekly between all spaces

We offer our members the support, infrastructure and tools needed to create the connections, momentum and recognition that will grow their businesses.

Above: Breakout space at the Shoreditch club.
Opposite: Meeting room at the Shoreditch club.

Above: The Bloomsbury club.
Opposite: The Shoreditch club.

Spaces

The brief for our interior designer Sevil Peach was to create a series of serviced work places – spaces that are fun, inspiring and sociable to work in, with the emphasis on a personalised and homely environment to encourage interaction and collaboration.

Peach has a strong view on how to create 'human' workplaces. Her spaces allow you to be inspired, work efficiently and relax. The interior architecture is very important; all the spaces are light, airy, organised and flexible. She uses a lot of colour, designer furniture and natural materials like wood to great effect.

We have a lot of beautiful pieces by Cappellini, Andreu World, e15 and Zeitraum. We wanted sustainable furniture that provides comfort while creating sleek, impressive environments that our members can take pride in when they have meetings with clients or invite guests. Art plays a very important role in our interiors as well. Our pieces come from the private art collection of our investor, Rattan Chadha, and they give the buildings colour and soul.

We have three branches. Each of them is unique, but all were chosen because of their buzzing locations. Our first building is on the Herengracht in Amsterdam and needed the most attention, but it has undergone a spectacular transformation. The 6-storey building was originally a social security benefits office. We reshaped the interior to maximise the available space, while keeping original features intact wherever possible. For example, the booths in the atrium where coworkers now work used to house small counters where people stood in line waiting for their benefits. The first floor was taken out, leaving an open work area looking down on a shared atrium. A glazed roof lets an abundance of light flood in.

The building we have on the Zuidas in Amsterdam was redesigned following the same concept. The exterior of this building is the least spectacular, but this only means that when you walk in, the interior makes an even bigger impression. This branch houses the largest number of members and is popular because there aren't any other spaces quite like it in the entire district.

Our latest location in The Hague is known as 'The Red Elephant'. The name comes from the head of an elephant which is to be found on the front of the tower on the building's facade. The elephant is not red, but the bricks of the exterior are.

One day, we hope to expand. Coworkers will walk into Spaces locations in London or New York but, wherever they are in the world, we want to them to thrive off the same vibrant metropolitan energy and to feel instantly at home.

Frederique Keuning, Co-Founder

Location	Herengracht, Amsterdam; Zuidas, Amsterdam; The Hague, Netherlands
Founders	Martijn Roordink and Frederique Keuning
Size	6,000 m² (Herengracht), 17,500 m² (Zuidas), 8,500 m² (The Hague)
Date opened	October 2008 (Herengracht), March 2010 (Zuidas), April 2013 (The Hague)
No. of workers	Approx. 1,000 within all spaces

Opposite: Booths in the Atrium of Herengracht where coworkers now sit used to be small counters where people stood in line for their benefits; lighting by Tom Dixon.

We wanted sustainable furniture that provides comfort while creating sleek, impressive environments that our members can take pride in when they have meetings with clients or invite guests.

Above: Lighting by Tom Dixon and seating by E15 in a breakout space in Herengracht.
Opposite: Lighting by FLOS in Zuidas.

Following Spread
Top left: Chairs by Andreu World and sofa by Josef Frank in a Clubroom in Herengracht.
Bottom left: Shared atrium space in Herengracht.
Top right: Table by Vitra and chairs by Cappellini in a meeting room in Herengracht.
Bottom right: Shelf system by MUUTO in a breakout space in Zuidas.

LOFFICE

In every office we have a specific style that we chose carefully. Each was designed by the Szupernova Design Group. Our building in Budapest was once a printing company serving the nearby music academy. Now, it's a stylish loft and home to a number of coworkers. With bold graphic art on the walls and exposed industrial features, we wanted to show how machines and people can live together – how they cooperate in everyday life. We tried to retain as many original features and as much history as possible. In our quest to be eco-friendly, we made furniture from recycled materials and found new uses for old pieces of equipment.

Our space in Vienna, situated in the 7th district, the quarter for creative people, was once a shoe factory. We wanted to emphasise the family nature of our business and create a homely vibe, so we renovated old family furniture. For example, the sofa once belonged to Kata and Anna's grandmother.

Since this office provides business solutions for both Austrian and Hungarian entrepreneurs, we wanted the style to express the freedom that we provide for them and also the connection between the two countries. Following the slogan that 'creative ideas need creative space', we kitted the place out with creative furniture. For example, coworkers can take down their notes on a blackboard in our meeting room called 'School'. In our other meeting room, our highlight is a table covered with a Swiss map.

LOFFICE is a community for those who are ready to escape from their isolated living-rooms; those who prefer working alongside peers in an organised and inspiring environment. We attract people from the creative sector who are willing to share their ideas with the community.

Csilla Dömötör, Community Manager, LOFFICE Coworking Budapest

Location	Budapest, Hungary; Vienna, Austria
Founders	Kata Klementz and Anna Klementz
Size	LOFFICE Coworking Budapest: 280 m²; LOFFICE Mini: 220 m²; LOFFICE Sas: 276 m²; LOFFICE Coworking Vienna: 350 m²
Date opened	January 2009 (LOFFICE Coworking Budapest), December 2010 (LOFFICE Mini), May 2011 (LOFFICE Sas), September 2011 (LOFFICE Coworking Vienna)
No. of workers	LOFFICE Coworking Budapest: 30; LOFFICE Mini: 15; LOFFICE Sas: 10; LOFFICE Coworking Vienna: 20

Opposite: A table covered with a Swiss map.

LOFFICE is a community for those who are ready to escape from their isolated living-rooms; those who prefer working alongside peers in an organised and inspiring environment.

Duke Studios

Inspired by the fun workspaces created by much larger organisations such as Google, Pixar and Innocent Smoothies, we wanted individuals and small businesses in Leeds to have access to a similarly creative, exciting work environment, but without having to be an employee of a big brand.

There are lots of interesting features in Duke Studios, but our Cardboard Studio structures are probably the most striking. We designed and developed the concept in-house, and then British manufacturer Dufaylite cut our design from Ultra Board material. The pieces arrive to us flat-packed and we popped the components out from sheets – a bit like an Airfix model kit – and slotted the elements together, assembling the structures without any nails, glue or screws.

Our building used to be a cloth mill but, unfortunately, it was used as an office before we moved in and all of the original features had either been removed or covered with plasterboard. We've knocked down walls to reclaim the original floor plan, but because of tight budget restrictions our design has had to adapt to many of the existing features. We embraced some original wood panelling that we found in one of the rooms and made our Not Bored Room, a space filled with little snippets of our fictitious Duke's life and the colourful history of Duke Studios.

Duke Studios is interesting, fun and exciting and so are all of our members. We have deliberately engineered a collaborative working environment that provides everything a creative business needs to survive and succeed. We then make sure that these opportunities are available to as many people as possible.

The design would have been pretty similar wherever we had chosen to set up Duke Studios, but we really wanted to find a space in a city centre location, which we've managed to do. This means we're a cog in a much bigger creative machine, situated alongside the likes of the BBC, The Northern Ballet and The West Yorkshire Playhouse as well as lots of other vibrant businesses in the creative heart of Leeds.

James Abbott-Donnelly, Co-Founder

Location	Leeds, UK
Founders	James Abbott-Donnelly and Laura Wellington
Size	650 m²
Date opened	January 2012
No. of workers	Currently has 49 members (10 studios, 8 permanent desks, 30+ coworking spaces)

Opposite: Detail of the kitchen area.
Above: Cardboard Studio structures.

MAKERS

Our inspiration came from the original 'makers' – the manual workers of yesteryear. We have highlighted the industrial era by incorporating handmade tools, repurposing sewing machines for tables, using vintage filing cabinets for room dividers, and stacks of old books for our reception desk. Essentially, we are making the old new again. Our colour theme has been to keep most of the space very neutral with grey, white and natural wood. We then allow the accent colour, which is currently yellow, to change depending on how the overall design looks and feels.

We really wanted to create a space that gives our members balance in life. Our bespoke desks really emphasise the juxtaposition between work and play. When a school in our area was replacing its gymnasium floor, we bought the whole thing. Our contractor (Lana's father, Greg) cut the pieces down to desk size, bound them with laminate and attached pipe legs. Now, our coworkers work on surfaces that were played on for years.

The Guiry Building was built in 1903 as a hotel and saloon. Over the years, it was used as a furniture store and when we were designing the interior we wanted to keep the look of a curated space that feels as though it's evolved gradually over time. Eventually, we plan to start selling our furnishings and keep the tradition alive.

Makers are innovators, creators and doers. They are urban Seattleites who enjoy a social gathering, be it happy hour in the kitchen or a launch party hosted in the space. We wanted to create a comfortable environment to encourage collaboration and discussion. With a flexible floor plan, we can create intimate spaces for team brainstorming or open everything up for lectures from industry leaders.

From the start, we were attracted to the open, airy space, the painted brick walls, hardwood floors, wood columns and non-fluorescent lighting. We kept all those features but enhanced them with beams, repurposed warehouse windows, sliding doors made from wooden bench seats and stained concrete. These industrial additions blend in and give us the professional yet non-corporate feeling we crave.

We are located just a few steps away from the historic Pike Place Market and the Seattle waterfront. Being so close to buildings that have been carefully preserved over the years has influenced the space's sustainable design. Most of our building supplies were repurposed from the space or local buildings and a majority of our furniture is either vintage or built on site.

MAKERS

Location	Seattle, Washington, USA
Founders	Caitlin Agnew and Lana Morisoli
Size	650 m²
Date opened	June 2012
No. of workers	70 desks

Opposite: Repurposed sewing machines for tables and vintage filing cabinets for room dividers.

We have highlighted the industrial era by incorporating handmade tools, repurposing sewing machines for tables, using vintage filing cabinets for room dividers, and stacks of old books for our reception desk.

Laptop

Our space is part of a complex of studios in a building that used to house an old print shop with a rotary press. Before that, it was home to a Russian clothing firm for theatre companies. It's a very inspiring part of town – rumour has it that in the last century the artists Jean Cocteau and Jean Marais used to rehearse in this area.

All of our furniture has been custom-made for us by carpenter David Martin, who created the desks and lockers with me, while our chairs are vintage. Sébastian Bertin from Les Enchaisés found them at the Salpetrière Laboratories, Cité Internationale and the Faculté de médecine Paris Descartes library. Some of them still have balls of chewing gum under the seats that were probably stuck there by students in the 1970s!

When we were creating this space, we were inspired by libraries and warehouses in London and Brooklyn. Visitors say this place has a refreshingly calm atmosphere. When you're here, you feel as though you are abroad – perhaps in London, New York or Tokyo – but we're still in Paris. Coworking is a relatively new concept in France, so I wanted people to enter this space and feel as though they are in a separate, exotic environment. We work here, but it really feels like a live/work place.

This is a vibrant, lively destination where passionate, artistic people gather. Here at Laptop, we seem to attract like-minded souls, so we all bounce ideas off each other and influence one another in a really positive way. The neighbours are writers, photographers, creative directors – even a famous aerialist who designed the aerial choreography for Wim Wenders' film *Wings of Desire*.

Pauline Thomas, Founder

Location	Paris, France
Founder	Pauline Thomas
Size	110 m²
Date opened	February 2012
No. of workers	Currently has 60 members (including 17 desks, 12 residents, 5 nomads)

The Office Group

Our London locations are a mix of open, private and semi-private spaces to work from. This workspace formula guides the layout and structure, but each location is distinctively styled to complement the rest of the building and the local area.

Exposed ceilings and boxed areas give Euston an industrial rawness, but the quality of the joinery and the soft furnishings balance this to create areas with a strong energy and sense of activity throughout. In Euston the colour palette is muted, and the floor finishing is softened with feature lighting (mixed in with traditional office fittings) to get the mood right. Typically, the people who work here are from the technology and creative sectors, from a mix of startups and more established businesses.

Warnford Court is a period building from the early 19th century and was at one point an extension to the Bank of England housing the offices of the Stock Exchange. The building oozes character, which we've considered in the use of dark wood and eclectic furnishings. We've sought to juxtapose a modern, contemporary finish within this heritage setting.

The Euston building was designed in the 1960s by architect Richard Seifert, who was known for creating robust Brutalist structures. The hexagonal design which can be seen in elements of the original building's facade have been repeated internally, such as with our feature steel wall. There are some fantastic views and we designed the open areas to directly benefit from them (rather than the smaller or private working areas).

We have an aversion to suspended ceilings with metal or fibre tiles, so in both buildings we've removed these everywhere and looked to gain some additional height and reveal the original concrete soffit where we can. In Euston the mechanical services are now exposed. Where they look a bit messy, we've installed painted timber slats that allow access and soften the overall impact. In Warnford Court, the timber is tongue and groove appointed to the soffit. Natural wood and soft tones were used to bring warmth to the space and more vibrant colours were applied in areas where we wanted to stimulate creativity.

As a design staple we love Anglepoise lamps. They're a strong yet natural feature in all our locations, working as task lighting throughout the spaces. In Warnford Court, we have a series of wall-mounted clocks that are detailed with City-related pursuits, such as banking and finance, rather than stating time differences around the world.

Charlie Green, Co-CEO

Location	London, UK
Founders	Charlie Green and Olly Olsen
Size	Warnford Court: 4,366 m² (371 m² coworking); Euston: 2,880m² (743 m² coworking)
Date opened	November 2011 (Warnford Court); December 2012 (Euston)
No. of workers	200 across both spaces

Opposite: Booth workspaces at Warnford Court.

Typically, the people who work here are from the technology and creative sectors, from a mix of startups and more established businesses.

Above: Orange and purple colour scheme shown in the soundproof chairs at Warnford Court.

Following Spread
Top left: Feature steel wall in the lounge area at Euston.
Bottom left: Anglepoise lamps in the Clubroom at Warnford Court.
Top right: Clubroom at Euston.
Bottom right: Drop-in workspaces at Euston.

Above: The Apartment at Warnford Court.

WeWork

We don't have a particular style, but we try to make spaces in which people feel happy and comfortable – places that inspire creativity and connection. At a fundamental level, the spaces have to support and empower the success of our members, and connected people are bound to be more successful.

I really love the library lounge area we have in our Hollywood building. It has a fireplace, which seems counter-intuitive for an office building in LA – but we love to do little quirky, unexpected things to give people a reason to think or perhaps inspire them to think differently.

We have ten buildings. Each has a unique history and a different construction, which we try to respond to. We have torn away layers and layers of disgusting carpeting, plasterboard and ceiling tiles in order to find the structure – the honesty – of the buildings. In every case, we've discovered amazing things that were hidden, whether it's an old wood floor that retains the markings of a hundred years of industrial use or a cast iron column with a unique form.

One of the most surprising things we uncovered was the original ceiling in our Midtown building in New York. It's located next door to the Empire State Building, and most office build-outs in the area have a corporate feel, which we were trying to avoid. When we found an old plaster ceiling with peeling paint, it became the thing I wanted to build around to create a space with warmth and depth of character. It had been covered for the past 50 years, so it wasn't in good shape. Covering it again would have been the easy thing to do, but exposing it completely changed the feeling of the interior space for the better.

We're a diverse community. While we do have certain floors dedicated to particular business types, we're not focused on any specific industry. Take a walk through one of our buildings and you'll encounter just about every business you can think of. This eclectic mix inspires curiosity, which leads to meaningful connections.

The neighbourhood a building is in certainly influences our design. There's no denying that Midtown New York is very different from the Meat Packing District, and it would be weird if the buildings in those two different areas were exactly the same. We always start our design process with a discussion of what we want the vibe to be, and the appropriate feel is greatly influenced by the surrounding context.

Miguel McKelvey, Co-Founder and Chief Creative Officer

Location	Manhattan, New York; San Francisco and Los Angeles, California, USA
Founders	Adam Neumann and Miguel McKelvey
Size	56,300 m² (across all locations)
Date opened	March 2010 – July 2013
No. of workers	6,401 (across all locations)

Opposite top: Breakout space in Los Angeles.
Opposite bottom: SoHo, New York.

We love to do little quirky, unexpected things to give people
a reason to think or perhaps inspire them to think differently.

Above: Kitchen area in Midtown, New York.

Above: Meeting rooms in the Meatpacking District, New York.

Above: Breakout space in SoHo West, New York.
Opposite top: Breakout space in the Meatpacking District, New York.
Opposite bottom: SoMa, San Francisco.

Spacecubed

Spacecubed was designed by Whisperin' Smith and is made using 75 per cent recycled materials, including old shipping pallets that have been crafted into desks and a 'chill out' hut. We wanted to encourage sustainability in Perth and we've included plenty of plants, too, to bring natural elements into the space.

To separate the various areas within the building, recycled window frames and stained-glass panes have been used. As the glass is clear and the window frames are no more than three metres high, they divide up the space without creating a sense of seclusion. Two wooden huts provide a breakaway space with informal beanbag seating where teams can unwind and chat.

Our site was once the Reserve Bank of Australia and was home to much of the gold in Western Australia. While the bank has since relocated, we still have the vault that we use as a spacious meeting or workshop room. It would have cost three million dollars to remove it! A smaller control room has been turned into a phone booth for private phone calls.

The space is for coworking, collaboration and innovation. The community is a diverse mix of people, made up of social and environmental entrepreneurs, technology and creative startups, and government and corporate innovation project teams. We believe that real progress comes from co-locating a varied range of people, sectors and organisations.

The space has been shaped by the community of people who use it and it has evolved organically over time. Rather than merely giving the coworkers what we thought they needed, we listened to the community members who provided ongoing feedback, then refined the design with this in mind.

Brodie McCulloch, Co-Founder

Location	Perth, Australia
Founder	Brodie McCulloch
Size	550 m²
Date opened	March 2012
No. of workers	Currently has 150 members (80 desks, 1 event space, 2 meeting rooms)

Opposite: Recycled stained-glass panes.
Above: Desks using old shipping pallets.

We wanted to encourage sustainability in Perth and we've included plenty of plants, too, to bring natural elements into the space.

Above: The 'chill out' hut made from old shipping pallets.

Opposite: The Vault meeting room.

port-of-entry

The studio provides a platform to allow young creatives to work, develop and share ideas within a central London location. port-of-entry also hosts a series of workshops, talks and exhibitions, where the walls become a canvas for fresh ideas and new ways of thinking. It's a real Petri dish for creativity.

The full history of our building is unknown. Some elements date back to the 1890s and we believe it was a textile sweatshop in the 1940s. Shoreditch went through a period of depression, leaving the premises vacant for a number of years. In 1997, my father Feyaz Mustafa opened the El Paso restaurant here, and port-of-entry is now in the basement. This family business, now run and owned by my brother Osman, has traded for the past 15 years, while the surrounding area developed.

To design the space, decades of paint and plaster were removed to reveal original features, from glazed tiles (once part of a series of toilet cubicles) to a Victorian counterweight. We gathered furniture from an array of sources, including antique fairs and house clearances. Friends, relatives and regular users of the space have donated pieces to us and it has a welcoming, familiar feel. Vintage furniture can trigger emotions linked to childhood, creating a sense of comfort, safety and fun. We have an amazing wall mural installation created by illustrator and animator Paul Layzell.

We are located in the heart of Shoreditch, East London. This area of the city is the epicentre of all things creative. The space has been made to accommodate the needs and ideals of those who live, work and aspire to be here. Our members are all gifted young people who have shown their talent and determination to succeed in the creative industries. We are merely a catalyst to their success.

Ziya Mustafa, Co-Founder

Location	London, UK
Founders	Christopher Richard Hall, Ziya Mustafa and Osman Mustafa
Size	190 m²
Date opened	November 2012
No. of workers	Currently has 44 members (desks are offered on a first come, first served basis each day)

Directory

BLINKBLINK
Gerichtstraße 25
D–13347 Berlin, Germany
mail@blinkblink.de
blinkblink.de

CENTRAL WORKING
11–13 Bayley Street
Bedford Square
London WC1B 3HD, UK
hi@centralworking.com
centralworking.com

CREATIVE LOUNGE MOV
Shibuya 2–21–1 8F (Hachi)
Shibuya Hikarie Building
Shibuya Ward
Tokyo, Japan
info@shibuyamov.com
shibuyamov.com

DCOLLAB
C/ San Joaqíun, Malasaña
28004 Madrid, Spain
hello@dcollab.com
dcollab.com

DUKE STUDIOS
1st Floor Munro House
Duke Street
Leeds LS9 8AG, UK
james@duke-studios.com
duke-studios.com

GOOGLE CAMPUS
4–5 Bonhill Street
London EC2A 4BX, UK
campuslondon.com

THE HIVE
21st Floor, The Phoenix Building
No. 23 Luard Road
Wan Chai, Hong Kong
info@thehive.com.hk
thehive.com.hk

THE HUB BERGEN
Holmedalsgården 3
5003 Bergen, Norway
bergen.hosts@the-hub.net
bergen.the-hub.net

THE HUB MADRID
c/ Gobernador 26
Madrid 28014, Spain
madrid.hosts@the-hub.net
madrid.the-hub.net

THE HUB WESTMINSTER
1st floor, New Zealand House
80 Haymarket
London SW1Y 4TE, UK
hosts@hubwestminster.net
westminster.the-hub.net

JELLYFISH CARTEL
3191 Casitas Avenue, Suite 102
Los Angeles, CA 90039, USA
jellyfishcartel@gmail.com
jellyfishcartel.com

LAPTOP
6 rue Arthur Rozier
Lofts alley, 2nd block left
75019 Paris, France
welcome@lelaptop.com
lelaptop.com

LIGHTSPACE
30 Light Street
Fortitude Valley
Brisbane QLD 4006, Australia
hello@lightspace.net.au
lightspace.net.au

LOFFICE
55 Paulay Ede Street
H–1061 Budapest, Hungary
office@loffice.hu
www.lofficecoworking.com

MAKE
Level One, Al Fattan House
Jumeirah Beach Road
Dubai Marina
Dubai, United Arab Emirates
info@MAKEbusinesshub.com
makebusinesshub.com

MAKERS
92 Lenora Street
Seattle, WA 98121, USA
info@themakersspace.com
themakersspace.com

MAKESHIFT SOCIETY
235 Gough Street
San Francisco, CA 94102, USA
info@makeshiftsociety.com
makeshiftsociety.com

MUSES & VISIONARIES
201 S. Narcissus Ave, Suite 2
West Palm Beach, FL 33401, USA
hello@musesandvisionaries.com
musesandvisionaries.com

PORT-OF-ENTRY
350–354 Old Street
London EC1V 9NQ, UK
hello@portofentry.co.uk
portofentry.co.uk

THE RABBIT HOLE
22 Agnes Street
Fortitude Valley
Brisbane QLD 4006, Australia
hello@coworkwithcoffee.com
coworkwithcoffee.com

SND CYN
14988 Sand Canyon Avenue
Irvine, CA 92618, USA
sndcyn@gmail.com
sndcyn.com

SOCIETYM GLASGOW
60 Renfrew Street
Glasgow G2 3BW, UK
info@societym.com
societym.com

SPACECUBED
Ground Floor
45 St Georges Terrace
Perth 6000, Australia
info@spacecubed.org
spacecubed.org

SUPER + SUPER
7 Kings Road
Brighton BN1 1NE, UK
supersuperhq@gmail.com
supersuperhq.com

SPACES
Herengracht 124–128
1015 BT, Amsterdam, Netherlands
receptie-herengracht@spaces.nl
spaces.nl

ST OBERHOLZ
Rosenthaler Straße 72a
10119 Berlin, Germany
info@sanktoberholz.de
sanktoberholz.de

THE OFFICE GROUP
Head Office
22 Manchester Square
London W1U 3PT, UK
22@theofficegroup.co.uk
theofficegroup.co.uk

THE ORACLE CLUB
10–41 47th Avenue
Long Island City
New York, NY 11101, USA
theoracleclub@gmail.com
theoracleclub.com

VUKA
411 West Monroe
Austin, TX 78704, USA
connect@vukaaustin.com
vukaaustin.com

WEWORK
175 Varick St
New York, NY 10014, USA
info@wework.com
wework.com

Acknowledgements

We would like to give a big thanks to all the coworking spaces that have helped us put this book together, to Martin Glover from Foster + Partners, and to all our supportive family and friends.

Picture Credits

Jaala Alex Photography: 40, 43
Marianne Annereau / businessphotos.com.au: 150, 153
Diego Berro: 36, 37
Joshua Brown: 104 (b), 105
CHARD Photo: 12
Matt Clayton: 138, 140 (t), 141
Alex Colby: 146
Claire Culley: 86
Josh Elliot Photography: 8
Rod Foster Photography: 9, 10, 11, 13, 14, 15
Will Foster: 126, 127, 128, 129, 130, 131, 132, 133
Gareth Gardner: 25, 26, 27, 28, 29
Jenna Gribbon: 104 (t)
Nikhilesh Haval: 139, 140 (b)
the Hive Hong Kong Ltd: 46, 47
Lena Hyde Photography: 49, 50, 51, 52, 53
JAD Photography: 124, 125
Josh Kelly / Platform Photography: 78, 79
KOKUYO Furniture Co., Ltd: 94, 95
Rooman Latif: 16, 17
Sharon Ann Lee @ CultureBrain: 4, 31, 32, 33, 34, 35
LOFFICE: 118, 120, 121, 122, 123

Andreas Louca: 66, 67
Jacqueline McCullough: 80, 82, 83, 84, 85, 87
Gerard Mensah: 154, 155
Nils Olav Mevatne: 54, 56, 57, 58, 59
Anna Niestroj: 18, 19, 20, 21, 22, 23
Justin Overell: 38, 41, 44, 45
Tim Pauly: 142 (t)
Lynton Pepper / oo:/: 76, 77
Andrew Pogue: 6, 88, 89, 90, 91, 92, 93
Richard Powers / citizenM: 60, 61, 62, 63, 64, 65
Marte L Rekaa: 106, 107, 110
Victoria Smith: 68, 69, 70, 71, 72, 73, 74, 75
Michael Semmen / Zum LLC: 147 (b)
Smoke Creative: 42
Stewart the Urban Snapper: 108, 109, 110, 111
Guido Thie: 112, 114, 115, 116, 117
Pauline Thomas: 134, 135
Daniel Torrelló: 96, 98, 99, 100, 101, 102, 103
Whisperin' Smith / Ben Hosking: 148, 149, 151, 152
Alan Williams: 137
Tim Williams: 142 (b), 144, 145, 147 (t)

© Prestel Verlag, Munich · London · New York, 2013.
© for the photographs see Picture Credits, page 159.
© for the texts by Alice Davies and Kathryn Tollervey.

Front cover: Top: The HUB Madrid (Daniel Torrelló);
Bottom: SND CYN (Rod Foster Photography).

Back cover: Top: The Rabbit Hole (Justin Overell);
Bottom left: SND CYN (Rod Foster Photography);
Bottom right: BLINKBLINK (Anna Niestroj).

Prestel Verlag, Munich
A member of Verlagsgruppe Random House GmbH

Prestel Verlag
Neumarkter Straße 28
81673 Munich
Tel. +49 (0)89 4136-0
Fax +49 (0)89 4136-2335
www.prestel.de

Prestel Publishing Ltd.
14–17 Wells Street
London W1T 3PD
Tel. +44 (0)20 7323 5004
Fax +44 (0)20 7323 0271

Prestel Publishing
900 Broadway, Suite 603
New York, NY 10003
Tel. +1 (212) 995-2720
Fax +1 (212) 995-2733
www.prestel.com

Library of Congress Control Number: 2013938624

British Library Cataloguing-in-Publication Data:
a catalogue record for this book is available from
the British Library; Deutsche National-bibliothek
holds a record of this publication in the Deutsche
Nationalbibliografie; detailed bibliographical data
can be found under: http://dnb.d-nb.de

Prestel books are available worldwide. Please contact
your nearest bookseller or one of the above addresses
for information concerning your local distributor.

Editorial direction: Ali Gitlow
Text editor: Ellie Tennant
Editorial assistance: Luna Schmidt
Copyediting: Malcolm Imrie

Design and layout: Victoria Forrest

Production: Friederike Schirge
Origination: Reproline Mediateam, Munich
Printing and binding: Neografia a.s.

Printed in Slovakia

The FSC®-certified paper Profimatt has been supplied by
Igepa, Germany

ISBN 978-3-7913-4857-5

FSC
www.fsc.org

MIX
Paper from
responsible sources
FSC® C020353